UNDER CLOUDS & CITY LIGHTS

UNDER CLOUDS & CITY LIGHTS

POEMS AND ILLUSTRATIONS
BY
CAITLIN JU

NEW DEGREE PRESS
COPYRIGHT © 2021 CAITLIN JU
All rights reserved.

UNDER CLOUDS & CITY LIGHTS
Poems and Illustrations

ISBN   978-1-63676-963-9   *Paperback*
   978-1-63730-029-9   *Kindle Ebook*
   978-1-63730-131-9   *Ebook*

I've learned that whenever I decide something with an open heart, I usually make the right decision.

—MAYA ANGELOU

CONTENTS

	AUTHOR'S NOTE	**13**
PART I	**BEGINNINGS**	**17**
	WHEN WE FIRST MET	18
	HONEY AND GLASS	19
	TO MY PARENTS	20
	MICHIGAN JANUARIES	21
	A LIFETIME OF HELLOS	22
	DREAMS™	23
	ASSUMPTIONS	25
	SPARKS AND STOMACH BUTTERFLIES	27
	HONEYMOON LOVE	28
	PINK AND BLUE	29
	22	30
	BEFORE I LOVE YOU	31
	MONDAY	32
	BEYOND THE ISLAND	33
	PLANTS IN MY ROOM	34
	WHAT IS THE DIFFERENCE BETWEEN LIKE AND LOVE? AND A MILLION OTHER QUESTIONS I HAVE FOR STRANGERS	35

	OUR FIRST YEAR	36
	BIRTHDAYS & NEW YEAR'S	37
	CITY LIGHTS	38
	PACIFIC OCEAN BEACH	39
	!	41
	CARDBOARD BOX	42
	LUCKY	43
	DECADES LATER	44
	LETTER TO MY YOUNGER SELF	46
PART II	**THOUGHT CLOUDS**	**47**
	i wish i knew	48
	SOFT HEARTS	49
	HOUSE OF LIES	50
	IS IT THAT BAD?	51
	A DELIGHTFUL SPIRAL	53
	IT NEVER ENDS	54
	MY ACHILLES' HEEL	57
	VICES	58
	TO ALL THE BOYS I'VE LOVED BEFORE AND EVERY ROM-COM EVER MADE	60
	SUPERPOWER	61
	ENERGY	62
	ARBORETUM THOUGHTS	63
	SOUND OF SILENCE	65
	SUMMER NIGHTS	66
	BLUE SILK PILLOW	67
	COFFEESHOP	69
	SWEET NIGHTMARES	70
	NEVER QUITE RIGHT	71
	PAPERCUTS	72
	END OF THE NIGHT	73

	HOW LONG UNTIL I CAN STOP ASKING?	74
	MAGIC	75
	LOST IN TRANSLATION	76
	SHADOWS AND WHAT REMAINS	77
	UNAVAILABLE	78
	BOLD	79
	FEBRUARY	80
	RESTLESS	81
PART III	**TRIALS**	**83**
	WAITING ROOM	84
	WHAT COULD HAVE BEEN	85
	LOST	86
	FLOWER CROWN	87
	IT'S NOT YOU	88
	THIS MOMENT	89
	PAINTED TRUTH	90
	BROKEN WINGS	92
	MORE	93
	WORK WORK WORK	95
	LIGHTNING	96
	THE CLOCK STRIKES MIDNIGHT	97
	A POSTCARD FROM 2020	99
	24 HOURS	101
	WHAT CAN YOU DO IF YOU'RE ONLY ONE PERSON?	102
	BOTTLED	104
	UNTITLED	105
	THE ONE	106
	VERTICAL	107
	THE BOY WHO CRIED WOLF	109
	BELIEVE HER	110

	UNDERWATER	111
	TOO LATE	112
	OKAY	113
	790 MILES	114
	HOPE	115
	HOME	116
PART IV	**LITTLE THINGS**	**117**
	PLANE TICKET	118
	BROWN EYES	119
	SWEATSHORTS	120
	THINGS I CAN'T THROW AWAY	122
	THINGS I HAVE LOST	123
	AS SEEN ON TV	124
	TINY BLACK SCREEN	125
	BLUE BUBBLES	126
	SPACE	127
	BOUQUET	128
	CUT FRUIT	129
	LITTLE YELLOW BALLOON	131
	TWO CUPS OF COFFEE	132
	SCARS	133
	CLOUDS	134
	POCKET CHANGE	136
	CALENDAR	137
	ART	138
	BLACK CONVERTIBLE	139
	RUSSIAN DOLL	141
	PUZZLE PIECES	142
	CHOPSTICKS	143
	BOX DYED HAIR	144
	RADIO	145

THE WHITE TREE	146
GOLDFISH	147
LEFTOVERS	148

PART V   **ENDINGS**   **149**

A LOVE LETTER TO CALIFORNIA	150
FRIENDS OR STRANGERS?	152
RULER	153
WHILE THE WORLD IS ASLEEP	155
LAST ROSE	156
ALL THE THINGS I WOULD HAVE TOLD YOU	157
COMING OF AGE	159
LAST TIME	160
THE TIPPING POINT	161
11 PM	163
WHEN SHE LET GO	164
SOME GOOD ENDS	165
ROSES AND PEACHES	166
A WHILE TOO LONG	167
BAD AT GOODBYES	168
HERE WE ARE AGAIN	170
FADE INTO THE DARK	171
PARIS IN THE WINTER	172
TIMELESS	173
EMPTY NEST	174
OBITUARIES	176
THE NEXT	177
EPILOGUE	179
HEAVEN	180

ACKNOWLEDGEMENTS   **181**

AUTHOR'S NOTE

When I began writing this book and illustrating it, it was so incredibly therapeutic I felt like I could finally breathe. It was my self-care, joy, and journey of self-reflection that started two months into the pandemic of 2020. All my life I had wanted to write a book to share my own thoughts on the world, but I never thought it would be through poetry.

While I sorted through the feelings that came with the social isolation of quarantine and a college senior year that looks very different from what I both expected and wanted, poetry was there for me when no other medium could capture what I and others were really feeling.

Under Clouds & City Lights is a collection about validating your thoughts and emotions. We don't spend nearly enough time just feeling and sitting in our thoughts, and we owe ourselves the time to process even the most mundane and negative. I, myself, don't celebrate the positive emotions enough. What I realized is that we have to understand how we feel before we understand who we are. Little moments and things contribute to this and shape who we become at every moment. Our lives are messy, and we are imperfect, but that makes the story more interesting. I wrote this to celebrate how beautifully complicated we all are, and I believe there is something breathtakingly wonderful about how there are so many universal human experiences we share, whether we are under clouds or city lights.

Born and raised in Saratoga, in the heart of Silicon Valley, California, I am a college student finishing up my degree in business at University of Michigan - Ann Arbor. After graduation, I will be in business. I am a young working Taiwanese-American woman who, by most standards, has no business publishing poetry, which is exactly why I want to.

In my conversations with family, close friends, and acquaintances, I realized there are many small things and experiences that tie us together. Even if you and I are very different and come from opposing backgrounds, there are still universal feelings and times in our lives that we share. This book draws from my own personal experience, my friends' stories, and media.

I feel no greater joy than when I see people all over the world, especially young people, bonding over our struggles and inspiring each other. By wearing my own heart on my sleeve through writing, I want to inspire vulnerability in others. This book is for those who have ever felt like they couldn't open up, those who are going through some of their most difficult times, and those who want to find hope by looking into their toughest and happiest past experiences.

This poetry collection of 131 individual poems is a reminder there are so many beautiful feelings, moments, and things that will end and begin over and over again. I have illustrated the collection to reinforce this simple yet chaotic nature of our lives. This book is for you to turn to so you can reflect and feel, no matter where you are in your life. I want to acknowledge all the moments of pain, triumph, and everything in between. These moments continue to strengthen me and make my journey worth it. This book became a place of rest and reflection for me, and I hope it can be that for you, too.

I am still thankful for the day I decided to finally publish my work online and share what I love most with others. All the people who supported me when I chose to publish made this possible. This book and the others that will follow will be for you just as much as it is for me.

ONE

BEGINNINGS

For every end, there is a beginning. Sometimes, we just wake up one day and decide it is one.

There is something about beginnings and firsts that we remember strongly. They live in our memories more powerfully than other moments. Beginnings mean new possibilities, and the feeling that almost anything can happen is one we subconsciously treasure.

New beginnings often follow endings. It is a beautiful promise of another chance and a fresh start. They are unexpected and, sometimes, healing. In some cases, we were forced into the beginning, thrust into uncertainty. In other cases, we sought it out.

We almost always remember beginnings fondly but find them difficult in the moment. We overthink and ask ourselves, where do we begin? It is true that beginnings can be lonely, and firsts can be scary, but they will be a part of who you become. This chapter is about our beginnings, whether it is the first time we experienced heartbreak, laughed, dreamed, met someone, doubted ourselves, or loved.

For all our beginnings that we have been through and the many to come —

When We First Met

I'll admit I didn't like you
too much when we first met,
but at the same time,
deep down
I knew
we would be fast friends.

We found each other like
two drowning souls
looking for
breaths of fresh air,
opening up the way only someone could
to a stranger.

Honey and Glass

I once preferred to be like honey and glass:
Palatable, pure, a lovely thing stuck in the past.
For my lips to taste like sweet caramel and my doe eyes to twinkle,
Fragile, ethereal beauty dressed up in sprinkles.
Someone to fawn over or protect,
A voice so soft and sultry you could barely detect,
A laugh so light and airy the wind carried it like music,
A presence forgettable and private-label generic.
Illusions wrapped into porcelain boxes topped with gift bows,
smiles so fake to hide what they hope no one knows.
Little by little, the honey turned sour;
The glass cracked and shattered with each hour.
An awakening happened within my heart and soul –
Why wait for others to make me feel whole?
I am no doll, relegated to no shelf.
I am somebody who knows herself.

To My Parents

For growing up eating rotten bean sprouts and moldy rice,
learning how the world works with your hands tied behind your backs,
working toward a future dependent on tests,
raising yourself with no money while being doubted,
coming to America with no one but each other,
made fun of for an accent despite graduate degrees,
taking care of two children,
living across the ocean from any family,
missing weddings, funerals, and everything in between,
constantly choosing to learn new skills,
raising two strong women who stand up for their beliefs,
letting me make my own choices and mistakes,
never punishing me but showing me the way,
taking the time to listen and grow politically,
showering me with love through small moments
and actions.
I will always be in awe.
Thank you.

Michigan Januaries

Another somber, fossil gray sky,
cemented by relentless, intense cold.

This day feels like yesterday,
like last month,
like last year.

It's hard to remember
what it ever was like before.

A Lifetime of Hellos

Hello, hola, bonjour, dobrý den, 你好,
nice to meet you
how are you?

over and over again,
ending as fast as they began,
how many encounters are just that —
the first and only time we will ever meet?

An invisible string
brought us together,
and just as quick,
pulled us apart.

A lifetime of hellos
isn't so bad,
but I hope we meet again.

DREAMS™

A little girl in pigtails wrapped in baby pink bowties
stares at me with her big brown eyes, soft but fearless,
her dark brown hair bouncing in excitement as she tells me
all the things she is going to do by the time she is thirty.

She's drawn the city that she plans to rule over,
all done on white printer paper taped together,
holding Barbies and Legos as the city's people in her hand,
declaring herself not queen but President of her fantasy land.

She's learning to fly by repeatedly jumping off the bed,
debating sometimes if she has another superpower instead,
but catching with every jump a little more air,
any doubt in her mind she is not special is rare.

The girl laughs when some man tells her at the fair
she can't be both a princess *and* a mermaid, he declares.
But she protests and has him draw her in both costumes,
and she tapes up those pictures outside of her bedroom.

She writes fairy tales with her toys as her guards,
gives gifts to her parents and friends in thoughtful, pages-long cards,
wishes at 11:11 and searches for shooting stars in
her backyard.

Everyone tells her, *you have big dreams*, smiling
but doubting,
as she grows up, telling her she can't do this or be that,
hoping to convince her she was not enough.

But the light never left her big brown eyes,
the dreams drifted from her sleep into reality,
and she began doing all the things she said she would.

assumptions

How bold people must be
to see my name
or my face
and think
they know,
to project their idea
of me onto my tired body.
Tired of being told
I am the one
assuming.
But I know.
For all my years
I have been forced
to sit in my discomfort
across interview tables,
dinner tables, happy hours,
classrooms, my own room.
For all the times
I have been
mistaken for another woman
who looks nothing like me,
called names on the street,
stalked,
and all the while
being told
that it's better than being
invisible.
I was taught it was safer
to be nice,
to say sweet things,

than risk breaking the fragile pedestal
built on my weary back.
I have worked too hard
for too long
for my name not to stand alone.

Sparks and Stomach Butterflies

when you least expect it,
the spark returns,
lighting up your eyes,
and against everything you told yourself
you begin to hope again.

just when I was about to quit,
the butterfly entered into my life,
resting gently on my palm,
making me forget
that a day ago,
I wanted to crush every Painted Lady butterfly
and never see one again.

Honeymoon Love

Lightning strikes the heart!
Floating baby butterflies!
Sunsets, clouds, blue skies!

pink and blue

I have always felt
like pink and blue with you.

But there is a comfort in our differences —
my ribbons and bows
against your dirty tennis shoes,
my honey-blonde hair
against your dark red strands,
my nights out
against your studio apartment stays.

We grew up
inside the same four walls,
dancing to the same songs,
playing the same piano,
eating the same food,
but

there is even more comfort
in learning from you,
in you watching me grow,
and in having you as my sister.

22

too young
to know what you're doing,
too old
to be forgiven for that.

too young
to feel like an adult,
too old
to not be considered one.

first jobs, big life decisions,
and new beginnings,
but why does it feel like
we are going through so many lasts?

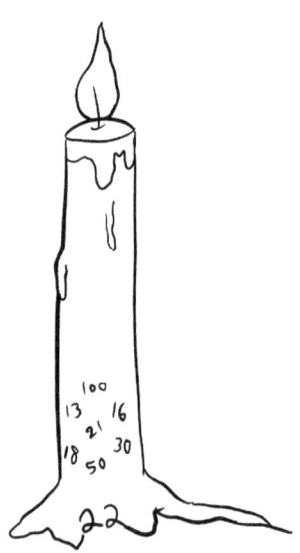

Before I Love You

There is so much to tell you,
so much I'm afraid to show you,
because it can be all too much and you might leave.

So before you give me forehead kisses
and drown me in perfumed words —
before I love you —
and let down my castle walls,

I want you to know
that I won't always be this happy,
that I can't help it.
There won't always be a reason.

You cannot always help me,
except to hold me tight,
and tell me you will stay...
even when I have tears streaming down my face,
or when I withdraw and guard my heart,
tell me you will be here at the end of it all.

Monday

A gradual dread creeps into the pits of stomachs,
the mood lingering in the air plummets,

missing the weekend of lounging about,
dress shirts are once again laid and smoothed out,

suit jackets are worn again to look well put-together,
in the office, small talk of light traffic and good weather,

inboxes full of emails to be checked,
many tasks from last week still to be addressed,

coffees are chugged and projects slowly worked through,
piles of papers waiting but too many meetings to go to,

everybody's least favorite day finally comes to an end,
not to be thought about until the next weekend.

Beyond the Island

Her untamed, sun-kissed brown hair flew with the wind,
her large chocolate eyes widened,
her powdered freckles creased.
She embodied the spirit of the island,
the volcanoes a spitting image of her fiery aura.

She longed for the world beyond her haven,
to soak in the glittering sights and cities
and to escape the simplicity of a planned life.
She wanted to teach others about her language, traditions,
and people.
She wanted to leave so she could come back.

Plants in My Room

This morning, the sunlight shines through
my ceiling window, bouncing onto my door.
A white glow fills my room, clouds drift by,
and I think about what this day will bring.

For now, I can pretend the world is
just the plants in my room and me,
the only things alive within these four white walls.
What is outside still remains a pleasant mystery.

Before I can spiral about all the things I have to get done,
I think about what I'm grateful for and all the fun things
to come.
Because, to get up today, I only need one good reason.
Sometimes, it's making my morning coffee,
or plans with a close friend, and most times it's worth
going out my door,
just to see what is waiting for me.

What is the difference between like and love? and a million other questions I have for strangers

we are not really strangers
if the same thoughts have ever crossed your mind

have you ever been in love?
why do you look up to them?
what does fear look like to you?
what are you looking for?
who were you before?

let's ask something meaningful
when we meet next time

Our First Year

All living things have a beginning,
and I hope yours was full of joy and loving,
and even though you won't remember this first year,
there will be memories made and adoration that you will
forever hold dear.

Your loved ones hold you close,
watch your fingers and toes
grow, rush to comfort you when you cry,
and promise you they would always be by your side.

birthdays & New Year's

the universe conspires
in expectations

two days a year,
to make all wishes come true

people celebrate less as time goes on
wondering where their life has gone

and the wish becomes
to have one more

City Lights

Ten years ago,
I danced under the snow,
falling onto the New York City sidewalk.
I looked up in awe at the Grand Central Clock
and skated under the Rockefeller Tree,
knowing this is where I wanted to be.

I promised myself that night
I would take one last flight
and make it my home
where I'd let it be known
I never forgot
to give my dreams a shot
no matter everything life threw my way,
so that girl ten years ago could see me today.

The lights are my stars and the streets are my signs
in the city that never sleeps.

Pacific Ocean Beach

PLACES REVISITED

I bury my toes into the moist sand until
they can no longer be seen.
I glance up.
The California sun glares
onto my dirt brown aviator sunglasses,
flooding me with memories
I'd prefer to forget.

Everything around is just different enough;
I can't shake the feeling
someone else
was sitting in my place
three years ago.

I focus on the kids
running away from the frothy tides,
the high-schoolers blasting their music
and scaling the dusty graffitied rocks,
and the middle-aged couples posing for photos.

I look down at what I am wearing
and remember all the times
I've ever worn this dress before.

I hate it.

I lie back on my rugby-striped beach towel,
the warmth of the sand and sun
lulling me to sleep.

!

it is a feeling like no other,
when the spark strikes and transforms into
a childish joy so powerful you cannot stop,
when you get energy from it.

!

maybe it's listening to a song that hits different or trying a new hobby,
maybe it's meeting a new person or taking an inspiring class,
maybe it's reading a touching book or going to a breathtaking place.

you feel called to do it,
you live for the excitement tingling your palms and fluttering your stomach,
your heart rate elevates and you get out of bed the next day,
a little happier, a little bit more ready.

!

Cardboard Box

One box left.

The room is full of cardboard boxes, nothing
special about them. They have some black Sharpie
scribbled over their surfaces, marking where they will
belong.
Fragile is stamped in red on the side of some, just in case.

The cardboard boxes hold our entire lives,
whittled down to a few chosen, precious objects. It is all
very ordinary
and unassuming. There are old sweaters, rolled neatly,
blankets,
books, photo albums, an electric kettle, dirt and dust
included.

The memories are locked away in the cardboard boxes, only
to be reopened once across the country. Unpacked, they
reek of
comforting familiarity, changing their new place from a
house
to a home. Without its contents, the box becomes like
any other.

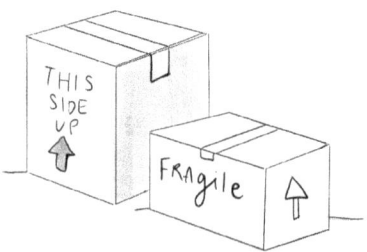

Lucky

We remember how they felt on our lips and skin,
how they smiled and we melted,
how hard each goodbye was,
how lucky we were to have the good times we did.

We remember how we gushed about them to friends,
thinking they could be the one,
how we had never felt this way,
how we had never loved this much before.

We will always remember,
with hope and love,
for we are lucky to have these memories,
and we are lucky to move on.

decades later

CHILDHOOD FRIENDS

decades later,

I expect we still be friends.
It won't be the same giggling in the back of the classroom,
passing notes under the table, gossiping about our crushes,
moving to different high schools and different colleges,
trying to pass our classes and get our first adult jobs;
we might not even meet in our hometowns.

But we will still watch each other cry and laugh. We will
still be difficult, romantic, ambitious souls, who remember
how naturally we once came together. Even when we don't
see each other for a year (or two) or don't talk for months.
We will remember how precious
it was to have met when we did, when we did not care
much about how we looked, who we knew, where
we worked,
and what we were doing, as long as it was fun. We will still
drive the other
because we all know who can't drive, we will still take the
goofiest pictures,
and we will still tell stories and make fun of each
other endlessly.
We will still
be there.

These are the people who were there in the beginning
and will be there in the end

when relationships fall apart, when other friends come
and go, when we celebrate our biggest wins and
life steps, and even when we move cities, states, and
countries
apart

decades later.

Letter to My Younger Self

You are so loved;
You will be more than okay;
Don't grow up too fast.

You are so loved;
You will be more than okay;
Don't grow up too fast.

You are so loved;
You will be more than okay;
Don't grow up too fast.

TWO

THOUGHT CLOUDS

Have you ever turned on music or left the TV on to feel less alone? Why do we think the most in showers and late at night? What are those thoughts we are most scared of?

There are some feelings that cannot be encompassed by a simple word. They come frequently into our minds as thought clouds and often leave just as quickly.

Our thoughts are more powerful than we give them credit for. They infect our emotions and drive our behavior. The thoughts in our mind manifest in how we lead our lives, and our mindset shapes how we approach the world.

This chapter is about all the thoughts that have lived in our mind and the emotions we have felt, feel now, and will feel. We deserve to sit in our thoughts, feel them, and validate them. We also choose the emotions we want to base our thoughts in, so we can choose to base our thoughts out of love rather than fear.

For all the times we have felt lonely, chaotic, undeserving, powerful, free, and vulnerable —

i wish i knew

what you were thinking,
if maybe you were
thinking about me right now,
when the lights are off,
as much as
I am thinking of you.
Are you thinking about
how it might snow,
how beautiful the night is,
if the trees are the right burnt orange
when the sunlight hits them at an angle,
or are you thinking about
what the lives of the people
in the tall buildings nearby
might be like,
why albatrosses mate for life,
how to comfortably put your arm
beneath my pillow,
how small the bed is,
or could you be thinking about
what your future
will look like,
where you will live,
if you mean what you say,
if you really know me,
when to open up,
or maybe you are as scared as me
to think at all?

Soft Hearts

You cry at dogs reuniting with their soldier owners,
You celebrate the hardest for others' birthdays,
You give your everything to your friends and family,
You *feel* with every ounce of your heart.
Others call you sensitive or weak
But, my friend, you are not.

The softest hearts are the strongest,
They move everyone forward.
The soft hearts are why I believe in this world—
The ones who care so much they *have* to help,
The ones who get joy from being there for others,
The ones who fight for justice, feel overwhelmed, and get back up to do it again.

It is easier to not care —
To wall yourself up so high you never feel, admit mistakes or open up.
You get hurt less, it's true,
But you miss out on so much.
You miss out on the purest friendships,
You miss out on having passions you want to pursue with all your being,
You miss out on hopes fulfilled,
You miss out on so much loving.

So soft hearts, take care and know yourself.
Once you do, then you can take care of others.
A soft heart is not the easy path but I promise
the world treasures it and we are better for it.

House of Lies

How terrifying
that if someone
just looked long enough
they would see you
for who you are!

Could you,
an Imposter,
ever belong?

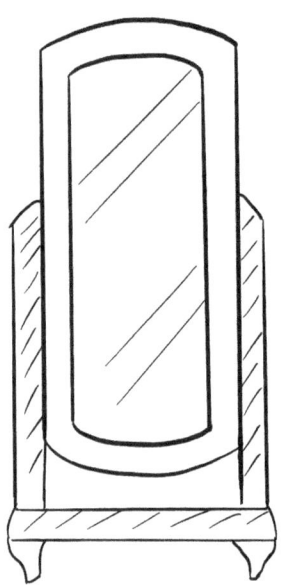

Is it that bad?

DE-STIGMATIZE THERAPY!

Why does it have to be
that bad
for you to seek help,
to raise your hand and finally acknowledge:
hey, I'm not doing okay?

It's not *that* bad —
but it'd be nice,
some days, to talk
to a therapist to say
hey, I'm not doing okay.

Friends and family try their best
but it can feel like a burden,
a downer, unacceptable, or
a great burning disappointment to bring up
hey, I'm not doing okay.

It is difficult enough for someone to peek their head
above water when they've been drowning
for months or years, made more difficult
by their closest ones not understanding
hey, I'm not doing okay.

Going to therapy is a sign of strength.
It is a sign you want change your mindset
and to improve how you are feeling. You take back your power
by not trying everyday to just stay afloat by saying
hey, I'm not doing okay.

If you know someone who is thinking
about therapy, let them know it's a path to healthier choices,
to be more vulnerable and discuss concerns,
and to deepen understanding because it can be overwhelming to
not feel okay.

A delightful spiral

Day after day,
                       night after night,
the same devil lifts its grinning face at me,
         laughing at the seat I still save for it.
It descends down the mind-numbing spiral staircase
         and sits at the dinner table with me,
howling at my fear of what is to come.
   I plan and plan, bracing myself for its contortions, and focus on the napkins while the stew rots.

I must know
how I can delight in the beautiful, uncontrollable unknown.

It Never Ends

It is not enough to write.
But to stay silent is to be part of the problem,
ignoring those who have no choice but to speak out
because it is their lived truths. It is a privilege to not care.
It never ends.
Exhaustion, frustration, and every emotion yet unnamed
follow each event. But the emotions must continue
to pour out of us because the world needs more outrage
that does not end when the media stops covering an event
or when the trial acquits yet again. It cannot end
because there are still people who
look at someone's face and think they know them,
think that others are less than, and think they can decide
whether others can live or die. To hear last pleading words
and feel and do nothing; it is a cruel world indeed.
It never ends. It is enough to churn our stomachs, consume us,
and still spill over.
The pain ends if we are desensitized, but
we cannot let it because racism does not confine itself
to Hollywood, the hiring process, or a century. It
never ends.
There has never been a time in America when it has not been like this.
Denial only suffocates and oppresses all of us. What justice
is in this world
we leave to the people we love when hate is taught. It
never ends.
Reinforced in the foundation of this country, the systems
that hold it up,

and the very people who are supposed to protect us.
It never ends. Because there is
no peace in jogging,
no peace in sleep,
no peace to even breathe.
Ahmaud Arbery,
Breonna Taylor,
George Floyd.
And the many more who were denied their life senselessly.
There are people in this country who must live this truth continuously
in their bodies and their minds. It never ends.
The doubts that society reinforces, relegating people
to fetishes and exceptions.
It never ends.
Even when they are tired,
tired of explaining why they are tired.
Our outrage and solidarity can never end, even as we are overwhelmed by the unfairness of the world.
Pretending we can boot-strap to fairness is the biggest lie.
No matter what they tell you, it *is* unfair.
It is a lie if you just work hard enough, life will be the same for you.
It is a lie if you just act good and be nice, life will be fair for you.
It is a lie if you keep your head down, mouth shut, life will be good to you.
For some, it is a lie. It never ends.
Words may not be enough right now, but it should not only be the burden
of those already oppressed, tired, exhausted, and overwhelmed

to speak and fight. It is for the rest of us to do the hard work
to learn our biases, systems, and others' lived truths.
We are not helpless.
We created, create, and will create injustice and we must fight it
one re-education, one conversation, one decision at a time.
Because it never ends.
Let's not pretend this was enough.

My Achilles' Heel

Perhaps my Achilles' heel is your soft smile
and sea foam eyes melting me
under the August sun.

Or maybe it is how I always believe what you say.

Vices

SOCIALLY PALATABLE ADDICTIONS

Are you addicted to what's in the bottle,
or really the bittersweet aftertaste of the booze,
or the lightheaded excitement, jolting you with bad ideas,
or the excuse to relive a past that is never coming back,
or the chance at freedom, a God-complex, and validated inhibition,
or the numbing of the pain, letting you escape the everyday,
or the fruity regret so you can let the days go by?

Are you addicted to the person you are with,
or really the idea of them,
or the emotional codependence,
or the snapshots of love, soundbites, and stories you can share,
or the escape from self-loathing and fear of the unknown,
or the crutch, fulfilling societal expectations,
or the intoxicating stability for you?

Are you addicted to self-improvement,
or really re-packaging toxic self-criticism and self-love culture,
or the cycle of fulfilling responsibilities and looking for more,
or the dependence on outside sources preaching quick fixes,
or the lifestyle to feel like you are progressing and doing something,

or the praise from others, wanting to be an inspiration,
or the chase to be enough?

These may be lesser vices we have come to accept,
but they are addictions nonetheless.

To All The Boys I've Loved Before and Every Rom-Com Ever Made

I buy into the dramatic airport declarations of love,
the marching band serenades,
unrealistic friend groups that stick together,
the cute but quirky girl catching unexpected attention.

I buy into the glasses making someone beautiful "ugly,"
the trip to Paris solving all problems,
the evil ex, the kissing in the pouring rain,
the best friend who does nothing but give love advice.

I buy into the beautiful woman made relatable by being clumsy,
people who have odd jobs but can afford a stunning apartment,
stereotyped sidekicks, the obvious Not The One,
the wedding breakups and dancing.

I buy into the soulmates who meet once and are separated by accident,
who realize suddenly all they ever needed was each other,
who forgive despite being horrible together,
all swept under the rug by grandiose romantic gestures and firework kisses.

I buy into it every time because
what would a life be without love?

Superpower

There are people we know who have
the charisma to bring the whole friend group together,
presence to command the room with a single word,
talent to induce tears that feel like daggers on cue,
voices that make hearts flutter and bring crowds to
their feet,
genius that captures every emotion perfectly on paper,
the gift for solving mathematical equations, writing code,
and creating art,
an eye for fashion, quality, and taste that exudes glamour,
boundless compassion for strangers that ripples
into others,
a face and body that graces covers, screens, and stages with
a heart to match,
courage to do daring, death-defying acts,
a brain that builds rockets and discovers microbes,
deep awareness of themselves and quick understanding
of others,
and ability to lead honestly, reinvent, and keep going when
others won't

but the real superpower is knowing that you are enough,
in a world telling you that you need to be more.

Energy

feel the energy of every word spoken,
    every thought had,
        every moment experienced,
            every time given and spent.

            save the energy for yourself,
        for the dreams you've always had,
    for the times you will remember at 80,
for the people who will give the same energy back.

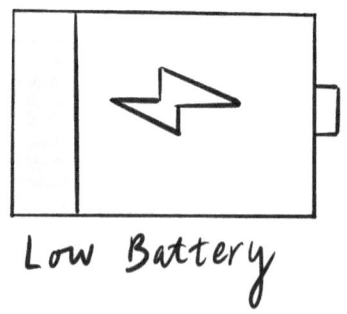

Arboretum Thoughts

What if purple swans existed? would swans be able to tell? would they care? the trees are so beautiful — I wonder if they ever get bored of their own existence; why are there so few people here on one of the sunniest days? I wish I could just focus on what's right in front of me, the delicate miniature beauty of these flowers, the squirrel's strange stance, looking straight at me, as if to ask — what are *you* doing here? "Don't you have a million thoughts you could be thinking, rather than about me?" Squirrel, who looks like a Fred, is probably just looking for his next meal.

Fred has dashed by and buried himself among the flowers; I wish I knew what these flowers were; in another life, I'd be a botanist and then maybe, my thoughts would be about the flowers; if I were a zoologist...; isn't it amazing that if I *really* decided that I wanted to be something, I could just you know, do it? perhaps a toxic thought that's made me need to always be busy.

Fred's disappeared from sight. I really hope reincarnation's real so that Fred could have a chance at the existence of a human; I think it's only fair. Then he can remember this day just as well as me and come up with a more efficient process for collecting nuts than in his tiny hands.

A couple is chatting behind me; it's just me and them in this large patch of grass, surrounded by chirping, distant passerby, and a very baby blue sky; no real clouds today; only a distant plane roams by that at night I would mistake for a star; it leaves a trail of white streaks, fake clouds that in some rom-com would spell *I love you, marry me*; isn't it funny how engine exhaust looks just like clouds?

We are right across from a busy street with some office buildings, thankfully mostly shielded with the stretched limbs of yellow-green trees; again, if I were a botanist, perhaps I could tell you what these trees were.

I've discarded my running shoes in favor of my yoga mat; I plan on keeping my socks on because even though I'm on a yoga mat, I still feel a bit weird having my bare feet out in public without flip flops; Fred's made a friend now and successfully found food.

I wouldn't have been able to just sit in the quiet before, but now, I could stay here a while.

Sound of Silence

I hear
your silence
too loudly.

Make some noise
and remind me
that I can forget you.

Summer Nights

The hot air feels heavy on my skin,
the heat rises to my flushed cheeks.
I pedal furiously on my bike,
no destination in mind
except to enjoy this summer night.

blue silk pillow

my head is on the blue silk pillow, looking at you
while one tiny tear rolls down past my nose and onto my other
cheek. I don't wipe it away because in that moment
I know

I know
that all the tears that bled from my eyes
for much different reasons before
suddenly made sense

suddenly made sense
why I could melt into your arms
and under the glow of your loving green eyes, want to
stop chasing for the next

stop chasing for the next
because what I had been looking for
stood before me, holding me with the warmth of
unspoken understanding

unspoken understanding
that we are the lucky ones to have found this,
knowing we will always remember this time of masks and chaos,
not like others, for this

not like others, for this
feeling of my hand resting on yours, while we walk under
small town lights and drive to search for stars, running
from the rain
until we are out of breath

until we are out of breath
from laughing too hard at only things we know, our bodies
intertwined with the comfort of the kind of love that fills
you with
those moments

those moments
where time stands still, where you think
you can do anything because
my head is on the blue silk pillow, looking at you.

coffeeshop

It is not unlike me
                        to want to be surrounded by people
To be in both noise and quiet.
              A well-dressed businesswoman walks by
And I wonder
                        if that will be me one day,
Hurrying to buy coffee
            without the time to stop and read books
Rushing to beat the time on my phone.

It is not unlike me
                to want to escape to places oceans apart
To experience both city life and country.
          The young barista pours milk into the coffee
And I wonder
                        if that will be me one day
Tired of 60 hour work weeks
            with only time for groceries and chores
Looking for the next vacation.

It is not unlike me
                      to want to do something crazy
To feel both busy and bored.
                The line to the counter is out the door
And I wonder
                        if that will be me one day
Waiting in lines for the same things
     waiting for calls, signs, and breaks to do things with
                                  others
Waiting to live.

Sweet Nightmares

I am filled with a sense of dread
that this could be the night
I finally die.
I busy myself with worldly matters,
trying to edge away the thought,
but it is too vivid,
colorful,
detailed,
and mysteriously perverse.
Creative universes burst from threads of my reality
revealing places I have never been and
purposes I have never had.
I soar above skyscrapers, neighborhoods, and even outer space,
away from something or someone
on a mission so dire that nothing else matters.
I remember
I am asleep.
This is the hundredth person I've saved this year,
the thirtieth run-through of this house to forest scenario.
Each night brings a twist,
an adventure so wild it can only be imagined.
I become a hero, unconfined by the laws of physics,
saving the world or a life,
sometimes my own.
Every refresh helps
to process an unjust world,
to seek answers to meditate on,
to connect with buried memories
and finally, to live without bounds.

Never Quite Right

This nagging feeling grows in me.
I never know if I'm doing things quite right.
Why does everyone else seem to know what they're doing?
   How does everyone seem to have it all together?
      How do they have the time to be everywhere?
         How do I know when I'm finally doing things right?

papercuts

*why do the shallow papercuts
you forgot you had
hurt the most?*

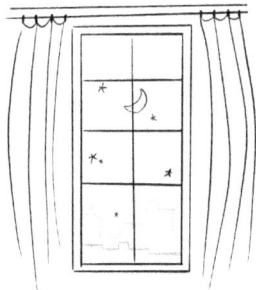

End of the Night

It hits me like a wave.
I lie on the bed, no longer feeling brave;
my breath, chest, and legs grow heavy.
My vision blurs as I count to three.
I run free into the streets,
anything to distract from my heartbeats.
The sunset, stars, and drives are no longer enough.
There is nothing left in me to act tough
as I empty the bottles until they line my windowsill,
hoping to catch a quick thrill.
But it's not enough for the darkness to leave,
even if there is nothing specific to grieve.
I stare in the mirror at my mascara waterfalls,
knowing that I won't be getting any calls.
I extend myself for others when they need me most,
a ghostly version of myself trying too hard to get close.
My head throbs and pounds as I wake up the next morning
and I go back once more to my performing.
I know how lucky I am,
but also that what I'm feeling is no sham.
There will always be more to unpack
but I want to know when the sky turns black,
that I won't be scared for the end of the night
and one day I can say everything turned out alright.

how long until I can stop asking?

At what age do people stop seeing a child
as someone to protect, someone just like them,
and start seeing their race instead?

How come the first thought when injustice is addressed
is that something is being taken away
rather than rectified?

Why are people so afraid of questioning and changing
what does not work
and hurts others?

Why do some people have to
tirelessly explain their own lived stories and
fight to be seen?

How does hate and fear grow
so quickly
and so senselessly?

Magic

I feel like I'm dreaming, and one day I will have to wake up and remember

seeing snow fall for the first time into a soft white blanket that covers the ground,
smelling the fresh crisp air of a cloudy morning after a storm the night before,
watching maple tree leaves turn golden orange and carmine red and fall in neat disarray,

feeling the warmth of a coffee cup spread through my numbed, cold fingers,
driving past a rainbow spread across a dark gray-blue sky, mirrored on wet pavement,
looking up at the twinkling stars on a clear pitch black sky near the ocean,

picking flowers to form the perfect purple-pink-yellow bouquet at the farmers market,
blasting old favorite songs through headphones while walking around aimlessly,
tasting warm dark chocolate cookie crumble melting under the tongue,

hearing from someone at the exact moment they were thought about,
sitting still for the first time, muscles relaxed and the mind clear,
and savoring every moment of awe that rushes in —

what a world we live in.

Lost in Translation

How many people would you connect with
if you just spoke their language?

How different might you be if you grew up
somewhere else or sometime else?

How might things change
if you said the thing you were most scared to?

Shadows and What Remains

Is this it then?

We try so desperately to shake the shadows,
merely getting by, surviving but not living,
waiting for the whispers to creep back.

When everything else becomes not enough,
when the people fail to fill the void,
when the sorrows creep past your lips,
swelling your mouth shut and blackening your eyes
into nothingness,

we are left alone with
what we have done.

Unavailable

my phone is off,
my energy not for you,
I might be in Costa Rica,
by the time you realize
I never stopped my life for you.

Bold

FOR THE EMBOLDENED

There is a change in the air,
in my movements, tone, and volume
— and yours.
Mocking anyone who dares call you or me quiet or shy,
for fear and care have left the conversation.
Welcome to a new world
in the quiet, confined to our homes.
A reckoning has taken place:
I have something to say!
And I am not asking whether anyone wants to hear it
Let it be known:
    I am bold.
    I lived with confidence infused with laughter.
    I was kind and compassionate but unfailing in
    my strength.
    I struggled vulnerably and connected with others,
    old and new.
    I did all that I could, as best as I could.
    I really cared about the world and, most of all, took
    care of me.
The world awaits that voice you and I have relegated too
long to our heads.
Why must you slumber until you see a sign or seize the
right moment?
Open your eyes, arms, and hearts,
Be **bold**.

february

I know I cannot love you
into loving me,
but I can't help wondering
if we might be thinking
of each other
at the same time?

Maybe that's why
I can't sleep.

Restless

I watch the trees whiz by
as I lean on the dirty train window.

I watch the clouds float by
as I lean on the tiny plane window.

I watch the houses speed by
as I lean on my dusty car window.

I watch as life flies by,
wondering if I am even participating.

THREE

TRIALS

When we think back on our life, we remember the key moments and experiences where we feel like we were challenged and weathered the storm. These are the times that made life feel like it would never be the same.

The details of these moments and challenges may be specific to us, but we are united in that nobody lives life unscathed. We lose people and innocence, and sometimes we have to fight for others and stand up for ourselves. We learn to draw support from the people around us, we learn from our struggles, and we build resilience.

This chapter is about the trials that make us cry, keep us up at night, and inspire the most growth. They can last seconds or years. They make for the best stories and, even in the darkest hours when we are not sure if they will ever end, we know we would never grow without this test. Our trials don't define us, but they do make us who we are.

For when life has made you feel hopeless, lost, overlooked, empowered, and loved, sometimes all at once —

Waiting Room

Sometimes I think I'd rather know,
but most times,
I'm just fine in the waiting room.

Here, I have all the possibilities,
strangers just as nervous as me,
and a little more time to hope.

What Could Have Been

No words pass between us as we stare at each other from across the table,
The silence screams softly, filling the air, yet we are left unable to express how we really feel, knowing time is running out, my knuckles whiten as my hands fist tightly, my head spinning with doubt.

If I said what I wanted, there would be no turning back.
Still I have found a needle in a haystack
and yet it's not enough for me,
people say only time will tell what's meant to be.

My cheeks flush like wildfire when I hear your name.
I know it started for both of us as a game,
but now I feel my heart pounding not knowing when I will see you next
and my breath quickens and hands tremble as I anticipate sending my goodbye text.

One day soon it'll end like any other,
and I will be left only to wonder,
replaying this lifetime of moments,
a beautiful ballet sequence stopped in its movements.

I hope one day we will meet again
and maybe it will be the right time then.
All we went through to find each other was not for nothing,
because, to me, it really meant something.

Lost

THE HARD CHOICES AHEAD

One side lures me with hauntingly beautiful redwood trees,
golden-yellow fallen leaves, and a ray of sunshine that peeks through
the brush at just the right place. It seems like the easier path,
promising a fairytale. But is it more Disney or Hans Christian Andersen?
I can't help but feel like it won't end well.

The other side taunts me with its siren-song fog touching the ground,
the menacing clouds gathering for a thunderstorm, and a path
obscured by rocks. It promises a difficult time filled with doubts,
but with the possibility of it paying off a hundred times over.
The uncertainty eats at me.

And so I pace in circles at the fork in the road,
afraid to choose.

Flower Crown

Don't forget to water the flowers in your head,
to tend to the weeds just as well as the sunflowers,

clear the ground when you are finally ready to plant,
till the soil and dig to prepare for long days ahead.

Check on your garden daily,
take care of them well, add nutrients

and surround them with warm sunlight.
Be sure to water them at the right time,

give them love, protect them,
and take moments every day to show off your
flower crown.

It's Not You

you are not for everyone;
the time will come
when you will be glad you waited.

Painted Truth

LIES YOU TELL YOURSELF

Muted. Greasy. Messy.
I stare in awe and disgust at myself and my art, a tangled ball of yarn.
I taste the beachy salt of my lies, hovering at the tip of my tongue, ready to unfurl and defend my last shred of sanity.
How *are* you doing?
I'm fine;
in fact, doing great.
The pickle juice drips from my mouth, somehow a little spicy, souring my face,
but I swallow that with my pride.
I step closer to the poison I concocted,
trying to summon the strength to resist. But the lies mix with my old perfume
and start to mock me in my sleep, knowing once I have begun I cannot stop.
Fueled by my denial,
they become a monster I can no longer control.
Still, I plaster a smile on my face and spout
social platitudes.
The melody grows burdensome,
the chorus annoying, the beats becoming not just
boring but
meaningless.
I'm sick of all of it!
I'm going insane!

This Moment

TO QUIET YOUR SOUL

This moment of rest
sits in your stomach with
disquieting stillness.
It is an out-of-body experience
that feels reassuring and
desperately peaceful.
This moment speaks to your soul,
a truce in a never-ending race
to get to the end of the day.
Stretch your arms and legs out,
exhale slowly and
reach into every inch of space around you.
Take these thirty seconds of rest
to sit,
to feel,
to let the world come to a stop.
Feel the strength rise within you,
rippling out.
You are at once out of control and
in control by
taking this moment to
feel your power.
Let your smile radiate
and your presence glow and welcome.
Treasure this moment
for there will never be this same moment again.

More

one winter day
i found myself
wanting More

i found myself looking at other couples
and wondering if they shared our pain,
or if i was alone drowning in a picture perfect love
going insane. Alone fighting for something
no one understood, for something i didn't even really want,
knowing i deserved More.

one spring day
i found myself
feeling tortured

i was a shell of my former self, dried and bled out
into an anxious mess i could have sworn
i was not before. More alone than if i was alone,
i had packaged and sold myself to become
some hopeless sounding board. When i realized
it would never change, that i could be free
and sane, the best reasons to stay
didn't matter anymore.

one summer day
i found myself reminiscing
about Before

i couldn't help it. i looked back on the thoughts
i had written in my leather-bound black journal that
had consumed me. There was a darkness to it all
i had not acknowledged before, a weight unprocessed,
goading and manipulating me to not search for More.

in a different time, i was a different person whose brain had
been dissected and split in half, studied until every
thought
and ounce of energy was drained, tubed, and funneled like
some odd science experiment performed where i was
Patient Zero: a ghost who wanted but couldn't even ask for
More

one fall day
I found it all
again

I remembered the pain and let it go, a sky lantern released
just in time as the earth cracked open. Euphoria and relief
coursed through me, as I looked down and saw what
was below.
I had never wanted so much rather to be alone. To heal,
feel,
and become

More

work work work

boredom kills those who
know the job is not for them,
no pay can keep you

work bleeds into life
until it becomes all there
is to talk about

getting through the day
eats at you until you ask
what will you do about it?

Lightning

Don't tell me about the fire poppy right now.

All I can see is the thick gray smoke billowing into
the skies,
making what were once baby blue and cotton candy clouds
an upsetting orange-gray paste, concealing an angry sun,
revealing an inferno.

The flames flicker dangerously, leaping and swirl-
ing together,
lighting up parched fields and redwood forests built to
stand the test of time,
too beautiful and proud to fail,
now lifeless sticks of charcoal.

I watch my memories burn,
stolen —
like in some bad fever dream,
we were struck by lightning and split in two.

I get lost in the madness that follows,
waiting for the earth to swallow me up,
for the fire to consume me,
but I am not so lucky.

The Clock Strikes Midnight

YOU ARE BUT SUMMER IN HER HEART

I could feel your breath against
my neck, your hand gripping mine

so tightly, as if you knew that when you let go
I would remember I shouldn't be

here. I turn to look at you, shapeless in the dark,
the moonlight illuminating just the left side

of your face. Your eyes are shut, your lips apart,
your breath held by the lightest golden strands

in the air. My heart races, and I open my mouth
to say something—anything—so that we can stay

frozen in time. But the fear of regret (and my pride)
is too strong, and no words come out and

I turn away. I rest my head against your chest and look up
at the midnight sky, filled with stars that blink,

mocking me with its movie moment
and mocking me with the futility

of it all. My white dress feels heavy against my skin
and I hold in a tear tempted to roll down my right cheek.

Our arms are wrapped tightly around each other,
unable to come to terms with the decision we made.

The wind blows through the monstrous waves
and prickles my skin, reminding me

that I will always remember this moment
for what could have been.

A Postcard from 2020

Home is the end of all boundaries in our new lives
and a place both treasured and hated when it confines —

the screens melt our eyes
and the body pains without movement.

We have never lived a year so strange,
so shared in burdens yet so alone.

Masks are our last defense, cloths once accessories,
now essential to keep us from the ground:

then the country falls apart at the thought
of having to wear them, the irony of breathing.

Hand sanitizer is the gel that we scrub on constantly
to keep us safe and sane. Another defense in an invisible battle.

Six feet is the room that keeps us safe –
distance that we must keep from strangers

for many months, hopeful that there will be some peace,
some solution or medicine that will absolve us.

But time is a race in circles,
the invisible virus emerging, waiting, emerging in waves.

In hospitals, machines whirl
as they pump air into lungs, but there are not enough.

People take tests to know
if they are safe. They go into rooms

with no contact. They lock the door
and suffer the noises for 14 days

until they are negative, at least twice. Everyone
carries their weight and pain differently.

The old hurt more, and the wealthy
complain in their palaces and islands.

The market with all the money crashes, but
the big tech companies thrive and grow.

Some go on like life is no different, and others
lose their jobs, families, and health.

We keep our distance and talk through video and phone,
hearing and reading about the world falling apart

in all the ways it always has, still knowing
that life will never be the same.

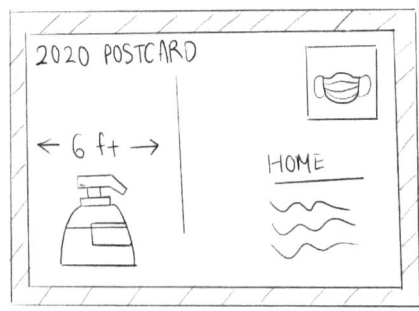

24 Hours

time moves differently
when I am here

in this time capsule
away from reality,

spending all 24 with you.

What can you do if you're only one person?

Every day, there is something.
With every piece of news, an ache sweeps across me,
engulfing me, tightening my chest,
and making tiny invisible scratches all over my body.

There are some moments in time
when we feel the world changing, the fires
raging, sea levels rising, rainforests disappearing,
countries closing borders, and people being murdered
in the streets and in their homes by the people
who are supposed to protect us.
When we realize
most people are living on far too little,
and very few living on far too much.
In these moments,
it can feel like all too much,
that this world is a little too big
to be made better by just one person.

There is a heaviness to this realization,
one we try to shield our children from until
they realize they or others are treated different
just for who they are. Then the same dark cloud
follows them around. But for all those who grew up to always take
and never to give, whose hateful actions can never be justified
in the selfishness, pain, and hurt they cause,
there are those who even if they were just one person
did what they could.

They moved their dollars
to where they would do the most good,
they spoke with force about injustice,
they built products and services to make
the world more connected, safer,
and understanding, and they made little changes
to live for the future they wanted.

So what can you do if you're only one person?

Live as if things could happen and ripple out
because of you.

Bottled

Nothing will set us free
until we confront the little monster inside our heads
that says we are not enough.

Untitled

you can make them say the right things,
but you can't make them trust you.

The One

Disclaimer: This poem is not about love.

It is about being the only One
in a room, melting in the shadows.
The One in a meeting, talked over and
interrupted. The One whispered about and judged
for being too much or too little. The One of something
it is so consumingly obvious to no one but you.
The One who
has to work three times as hard with unattainable perfection, swallowing
pride for fear of being seen as too sensitive. The One
enduring ridiculous moments.

Thank you to all the Ones who came before and to all the Ones now.
Here's to becoming the One to inspire One Thousand.

Vertical

FOR THE MOUNTAINS WE WILL ALL HAVE AHEAD

The trail ahead doesn't look so daunting anymore. The steep incline feels
almost welcoming, and the thorn-filled bushes, jagged rocks, and occasional red, white, and black striped snake do little to faze him. He makes it a game, jumping as if he were a frog around lily pads,
his drawstring bag lightly bouncing on his back.

He can't see the other side of the mountain and ponders when he will finally reach it. The peak is hidden by a misty, hauntingly beautiful fog,
but he doesn't look back because he already knows how far he's come.
Instead, he looks to his side and sees how little the forests he passed now appear.

On the other side of the mountain, she moves to adjust her sunglasses on the top of her head, tangled in her thin, light brown hair and laughs at the inconvenience. A moment of doubt fills her as the light dims
and the sun begins to set, but she takes a deep breath and pushes on.
She wonders if she has enough air in her lungs and strength in her burning thighs
to make it. Her face is flushed and she questions why she already feels exhausted

and if she is far enough along. Her ears grow numb, and she shoves her fingers deeper into her jacket pockets. She rests on a rock protruding from the side of the mountain and places her lips against the cold metal of her water bottle. She reaches into her backpack to reveal half-crushed energy bars and gulps them down. The dirt around her boots still has traces of ice from the snowy days before.

The silence of the woods descends upon her until a brown-capped rosy finch flutters by. Relief washes over her, as she sees the summit. She sees a man with a drawstring bag already there and hopes he is also just as proud as she is that they had the courage to keep going, no matter how long it took.

The boy who cried wolf

He was only seventeen, they said
Too young for the world.
You couldn't blame him.
So much potential.
But he was no sheep,
no lamb waiting to be slaughtered.
Not all mistakes can be forgiven
when he knew what he was,
a wolf only pretending to be a boy.

believe her

SHE HAS A NAME

They said
if she was a little quieter,
a little more obedient,
a little less slutty,
nothing would happen.

she had spent too long
caring
and hating herself
when she saw what happened
to her and all before her,

she hated all of it,
especially Them.

she had a power
They tried to squash
when she decided
she would not be buried,
she would not be used,
she would remind Them
she would not be forgotten.

They would know her name.

They would be forced to
confront Their arrogance
in the Hell They belonged to.

Underwater

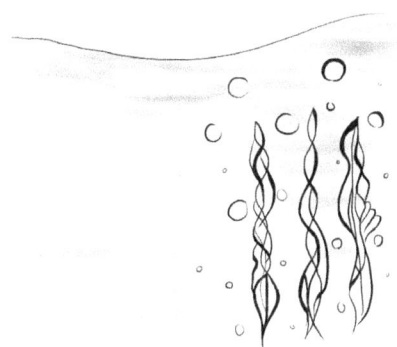

In this liquid world she became a silhouette,
dancing against the sun's beams, submerged
in the thrill of freedom mixed with tranquility.
She discovered she could hold her breath,
longer each time until the agony of
running out of air dimmed. This time,
the water touched her vocal cords and
she knew, she had gone a little too far. Her head
shot above the water and she gasped.
The bathroom mirror had long fogged.
She looked down at her reflection rippling in waves
in the dull, soapy green water of the bathtub.
Her body was soaked; her fingers pruned as she clung
to the cold porcelain walls of the bathtub.
She was alone.
No witnesses to her puffy red-ringed eyes. Nobody to know
that she had sat in the bathtub, underwater,
just a little too long.

Too Late

She wishes she could tell you
before it's too late,
that she still cares and loves,
just in a different way.

She might not be as happy
or as bubbly in that childish carefree way
but inside, she appreciates you
just the same.

She wants you to know, as her parents,
that she wishes she could tell you more
and that you'd ask but sometimes she feels
that maybe it is already too late.

okay

Under the harsh lighting
in the doctor's room,
your dark circles, wrinkles,
and frail body look different.
I forgot how much time has passed —
your hair is gone,
your skin is paler, and
your smile is smaller.
I have only seen you cry
three times in my life,
but I want you to cry now
so you don't have to
be the strong one
this time.
My tears come like knives cutting my face
and I try to deny
the possibility you will not see me on my
graduation or wedding day.
Even though you have lived without me,
I have not lived without you, and
I pray
that it will be okay.

790 miles

Seven hundred ninety miles feels further
when I know it is the distance
between me and you. I have wondered
when I saw others, how they did it, how they
stood the test of months and years
through calls and short visits. *How.*

But I see you through my tiny screen and
hold you in my arms each time we are reunited and
remember *why.*

hope

what
drives you forward,
in a world
where you can lose
it so easily? I hope

that you hold on.
There are good things
worth fighting for.

Home

I have moved away,
but I still call where I grew up home.
But I know one day,
I will have a place that finally feels like my own.

FOUR

LITTLE THINGS

―

As important as feelings and moments are to our lives, the little things that we own and surround ourselves with play just as significant of a role.

These little things carry emotions and precious memories. They can simply spark joy or convey a deeper meaning. The "thing" may be very small, like chopsticks, very large, like space, or be something that belongs to the world, like clouds.

This chapter is about the little things in our lives that tell a story. Just like how objects in museums have history and significance to them, a sentimental T-shirt can have its own story in your life. Just like how a passport means more than pieces of paper, we all have objects in our lives that mean more than they appear.

For all the little things that make life and us special —

plane ticket

one day I hope these tickets will just be stubs
beside old pictures and love notes,
but for now,

each one is worth more than the hundreds of dollars
I would pour into seeing you
just a little sooner
and a little more often.

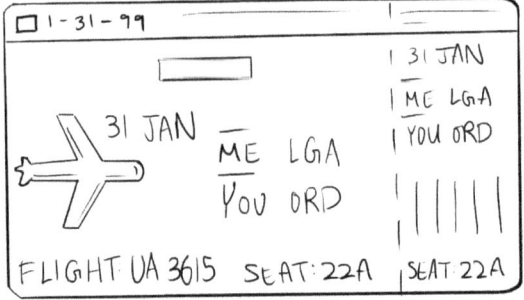

Brown Eyes

Muddy chocolate pools lined with sparse lashes,
flat thin hair, flat nose, flat chest,
hanging belly fat, bad tank and flip-flop tans,
matching unshaved flabby underarms,
freckles dotted to meet the foundation-caked acne,
no obvious jawline with a less-than-ideal side profile,
a million things to pick and pull apart.

But staring into her brown eyes while leaning on a messy
bathroom counter to look closely into the dirty mirror,
she can say she is learning to love all those things,
starting with those brown eyes.

Sweatshorts

TO REMEMBER A TRANSFORMATIVE, UNFORGETTABLE YEAR

At times I feel like an old soul,
snuggled between my dryer-fresh sheets and thin summer blanket,
a book next to me, a wine mug in hand, and
my laptop slightly overheating on my legs.
The world seems to still in my brightly lit room,
slumbering
in the cricket quiet,
I almost forget the noise of the life I had before,
before sweatshorts, virtual hangouts, and cloth masks.

As I sit here
meditating, journaling, and praying,
I remember that I am still the same. Still a sucker for a good romantic comedy,
still unable to commit to ab workouts and an empty weekend, and still
overthinking and growing.

I smile,
feeling healthier and happier,
even when I know no one can see it
under my mask, on phone meetings, and to myself.
There are many moments when I wonder what would have happened
if I did not get this chance to
sit in the anxiousness of an uncertain world,
finally feeling free.

I glance down at my cotton gray sweatshorts,
the pair on today's rotation, and think about how
this year might have saved me.

Things I Can't Throw Away

An objectively ugly, puke green turtleneck sweater - have I even ever worn it? / Hamilton poster with Gorilla tape still tacked on its back - I still love Hamilton, right? / "But First, Coffee" white mug with a broken handle - sentimental gift / mini football with the company logo of my former employer - nostalgia / a dried-up whiteboard marker - can't explain this one / old, stained, sea foam-colored pillowcase covers - for when I wash my current pillowcase covers? / a one-third full Black Cherry Whiteclaw - I'll finish it sometime / old card from someone I barely talk to anymore - still means a lot / two-year-old Clinique lipstick - still mostly unused / two cow stuffed animals - too many childhood memories / last year's history textbook, written by my professor - one day I'll actually read it / everything I should have

Things I Have Lost

3 pairs of earbuds / contact lens inside a bathroom sink / sleep / one boot / one earring / patience with unreasonable, passive-aggressive people / socks, always in laundry / hours on people who don't deserve it / money in the stock market / keys / friends / ability to run a 6-minute mile / innocence / pasta from burning it / interest in what acquaintances or strangers think / toenails / all of my middle school photos in my iPhone7 that I forgot the password to / important people / faith in the government / that one thing I really need to find

As Seen on TV

There is an indescribable joy I feel
when I see someone who looks like me on TV.
It is rare, few, and far between,
for Hollywood does not favor those who look, sound, and act like me
on either the small or silver screen.

Maybe if we all cared and paid attention,
we would not relegate people of color to sidekicks, caricatures, or tropes.
It has long been time to quiet the excuses
so that people can see what I see all around me —
Asian American men and women who are strong, beautiful people who live powerfully.

It is difficult to understand, know about, or feel for people you do not ever meet or see,
and that is the true power of TV.
We will always be more than the sliver others see,
but without good representation,
we are painted as rarely impassioned portraits to match what those in power think.
It may seem like a little thing,
but it's not in a world that would still call me a chink.

Tiny Black Screen

On/off, wasting away time
Mirror, contortion
Brain drain, lifeline
Addiction, connection
Comparison, influence

An intoxicating bond, liberating us
with the power we give it.
Indeed no greater contradiction
than the little black screen.

Blue Bubbles

Hi

                                          What's up?!

I've missed you
How's it going?

                                Great, good to hear from you!

Yeah, I am doing well too
We need to catch up more often.

                Yeah, work's been busy lol, How about for you??

Same. Let me know when you are free next!

                            For sure, keep me updated on things.

I will.

                                  Send me pictures from your trip!
                                    Sorry I'm bad at responding.

No worries, all good.

                                                Hang out soon!!

Can't wait

When?

Space

New days,
new realizations,
adjusting.
New habits,
new people,
growing.
New places,
new favorites,
writing poetry.
The one thing
that heals.

Bouquet

Pretty
flowers
wilt too

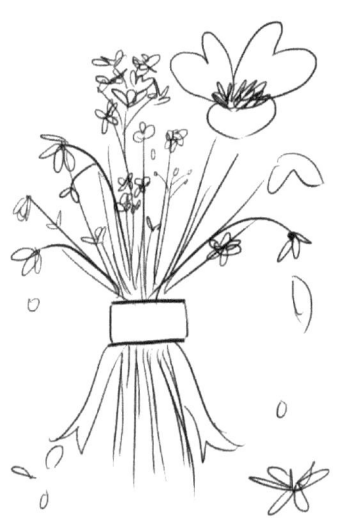

Cut Fruit

What is your parents' love language?
Mine is cutting fruit for me
and reminding me to eat it.

It is getting up early every day
to prepare and pack breakfast or lunch
after working late into the night.

It is bringing me to science museums,
reading me Roald Dahl stories,
and throwing stuffed animals in basketball hoops.

It is gluing the scientific method onto cardboard
for my science fair projects in middle school,
and rushing to the store last minute for a broken
gear piece.

It is spending entire weekends to drive hours to my tennis matches,
putting up tents in the living room to pretend we
were camping,
and filling my life with art, culture, and
WWII documentaries.

It is giving me the last piece of food on each plate,
telling me about the latest animal footage they've seen,
and writing supportive notes about how strong I am.

It is letting me quit things when I no longer love them,
supporting me when I put the cello away
and decided not to recruit college tennis.

It is wanting the best for me,
but always letting me make my own decisions,
and giving me the wings to fly far away

to new cities and other countries,
making new friends and new homes,
never letting me forget

to eat my cut fruit.

Little Yellow Balloon

The little yellow balloon
broke free from where it had been tied
and floated into the overcast sky.

It did not know how far it could travel
or how high it could go,
only that it wanted to see another balloon.

Two Cups of Coffee

m o r n i n g
one latte
no sugar
no cream

the rich earthy warm smell of early morning coffee
tingles my nose, awakening my sleepy eyelids and
enveloping me in comfort

a f t e r n o o n
an espresso
maybe some sugar
still no cream

the sound of a fresh cup brewing re-energizes me,
the rush of its slightly sweet but bitter taste sending
a surge of heat through my body

when did needing one pick me up turn into two?

Scars

I would
put my hand
on the stove
again for you;

At least then
I would have the scars
to remember
it was real.

Clouds

So still I forget they are alive. That I am alive.

How are the clouds so perfect
when they don't make any sense?
The patchy white ribbons float by the oval glass
of the plane, melting mountains and shielding
harsh-yellowed hills. Peering from under my hand,
I see their glowing edges dotting baby blue palette skies.
Sometimes, they are sherpa blankets and cotton balls
stretching across the horizon, leaking gold, orange,
and pink.
Sometimes, they are slate gray puddles splashed across a
growing raisin black canvas,
spilling defiance and an expectant air into the mood.

The casual beauty of their singular infiniteness,
the sky opening in a breath,
stops passerby in their tracks.

Two children picking furiously at dandelions in a fresh
green field lie on their backs, the wet grass bristling
their cheeks.
They go back and forth about what each fleecy pile looks like,
and they settle on a turtle battling a dragon.
Somewhere across the world, a girl runs to catch the
breezy thermal streams. Her hands pass through but she
smiles
and soft laughter escapes. The azure skies paint a shapeless
cream layer to match how she floats, wandering and escaping into daydreams.

Her mind settles on the thought that
out there, someone is
watching the clouds in wonder too.

Pocket change

Pocket change to be kind:
to give those bills crumpled in purses
or spare time away once in a while,
When it's given to those who don't have it,
it means more than we will ever know.

Calendar

my calendar
is a monster
that grips
tightly to my time,
tearing me away
from possibilities
and scheduling
my binds.

a devil's deal
was made
to keep my life
in white squares
but life in the dungeon
feels better
than anywhere else.

Art

blushing
and beautiful,
a heavy sadness
as the artist paints
what he can get away with
and the poet writes
about her mesmerizing chaos.
Must there always be pain
for good art to be born?

Black Convertible

Arms stretched to the sky,
Wind blowing my hair in a million directions,
the rush popping my ears and starting my heart;
Today it all makes sense.

I feel infinite.
I may be in a leather seat, but I am untethered to the world
with the roof down. I rest my arm on the car door, my
hand moving up
and down like a wave. I lean closer to the edge, popping
my head out to yell

I am free!
I can smell the salty ocean air, the musty forest soil, and
golden wheat fields.
I am moving, everything around me changing but
somehow
I feel at home. I have invited chaos around and
peace within.

Arms stretched out around my keyboard as my fingers
type away,
My mind pulled in a million directions,
the rush of getting work done pumping my heart;
Today nothing makes sense.

I feel lost.

Though I am in the respectable job I wanted, I am but tethered to the world.

I rest my arm on my table, propping my head up to see other cars whizz by.

I lean closer to the window next to me, restraining myself from opening it to yell

I want more!

I can smell the ocean, forests, and fields calling me.

I take a deep breath.

The ride has just begun.

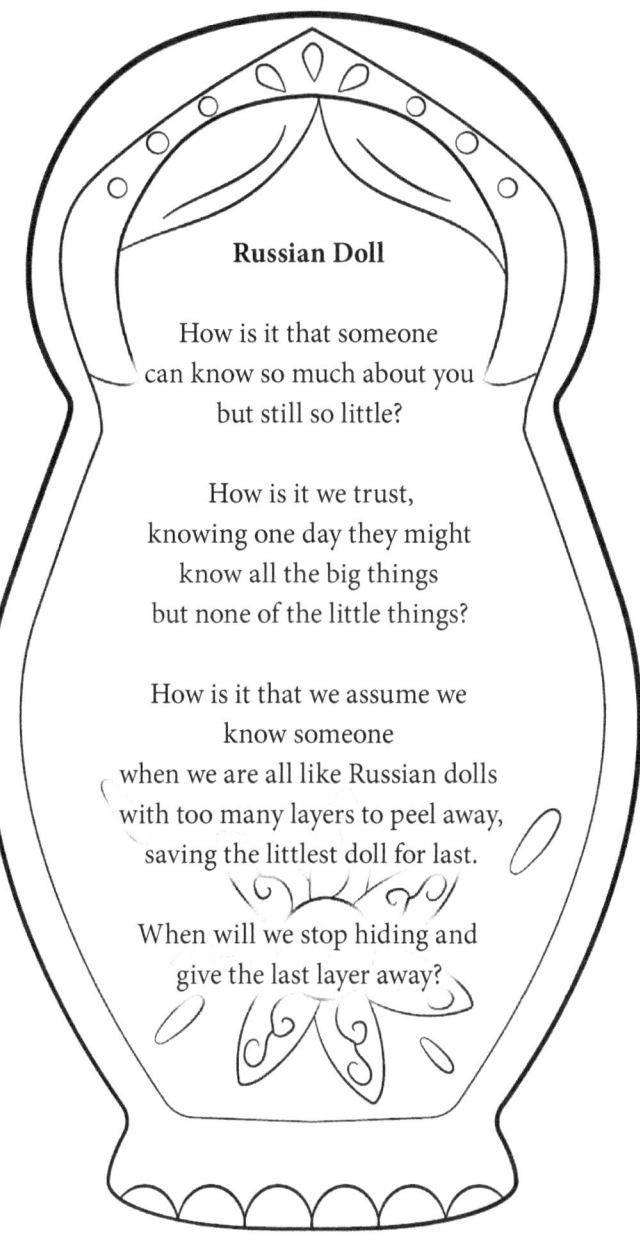

Russian Doll

How is it that someone
can know so much about you
but still so little?

How is it we trust,
knowing one day they might
know all the big things
but none of the little things?

How is it that we assume we
know someone
when we are all like Russian dolls
with too many layers to peel away,
saving the littlest doll for last.

When will we stop hiding and
give the last layer away?

Puzzle Pieces

I miss the feeling of everything falling into place,
like finding lost puzzle pieces to fill in the blank space.
When the edges fit together and the puzzle begins to take shape,
working on my jigsaw puzzles no longer feels like
an escape.

Even when my puzzle seems almost done,
I will still be searching for another one.

Chopsticks

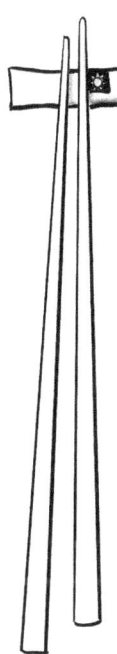

I never can hold my chopsticks quite right.
Good enough that I use them for every meal,
but not good enough to teach others.
It reminds me of how I am between two worlds,
too Asian for America, too American for Asia:
never fully accepted in either,
kicked, beaten, and written into submission,
and erased from history but not judgment.

A boat floundering in an ocean,
trying to bridge the chasm between being

Asian enough because of my golden melanin hue,
my parents' immigrant story,
and my affinity for Asian food.
Not Asian enough because of my freckles,
my perfect English, and how I don't know nearly
enough about my heritage.

Lost in between *go back where you came from!* and
being the expected expert on my parents' culture.
Identified by a country I visit only every few years,
identified by a face that comes with hate and
assumptions, and misidentified constantly.
It is no wonder
I feel like those training chopsticks glued together
at the top,
stuck between two worlds.

Box Dyed Hair

Bad decisions make good stories.
She sits facing her mirror, two boxes
of hair dye in front of her. She pulls on
her gloves, gets her bowl and brush,
and starts from the roots.

She sits facing her mirror, her new hair
draping around her shoulders. Her eyes
sparkle with a new energy as she looks
at herself. There is always some comfort in knowing you
can start over.

Radio

Our song plays over the radio,
the vibrations sending me back.
I don't change the channel,
because it doesn't bother me anymore.
It just reminds me
of all the ways
I've changed
and how far I've come.

I turn the volume up
and begin to dance.

The White Tree

The golden forest was covered by mist,
guarded by magic so no evil could enter.
Yellow flowers, golden wood, and silver pillars protected it from Men,
but in the middle, the White Tree stood, covered in pearl blossoms and bright silver leaves.

Many tried to destroy it with fire, greed, and worse,
and a few came close.
But the White Tree still stands,
a symbol of resilience, renewal, and strength among the shadows.

Inspired by my favorite movie trilogy, Lord of the Rings

Goldfish

some people are just goldfish,
flailing wildly when out of water,
desperate to be put back in what they know

        one day these goldfish
        might stop swimming in circles
    and realize the world is not just their bowl

leftovers

there are some things that are not as good
as we remember them to be.

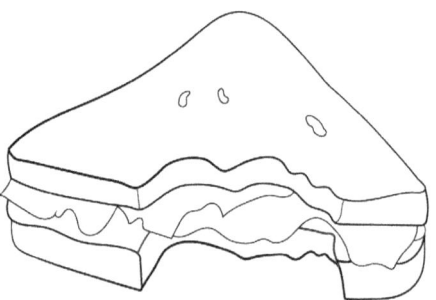

FIVE

ENDINGS

Nothing is more beautiful to me than endings. We all have to experience many lasts and endings, like the last time you talk to a person, the last time you are in a place, or the end of life, but these are such a natural part of living that they often feel more touching than sad.

Without endings, living would lose much of its wonder and meaning. We would treasure the little moments much less. We would take life for granted.

This chapter is about more than just the endings we experience in life. It is about the beauty, strength, and growth that comes with endings. Some endings are dependable, like the end of the night, and others are unexpected, like losing someone we love too early.

There are several endings I have not yet experienced and could not write from my heart, but I have written from seeing friends and strangers go through them. We do lose something in endings, but they always teach us something. For all the lasts and endings that we have gone through and will ever experience —

A Love Letter to California

I am sorry I am leaving.

I know it's nothing new, and maybe you don't care. I have left many times before without hesitation, with the speed reserved only for a girl felt confined by her hometown, foggy memories, and perpetual boredom.

I left without looking back because I knew I wasn't really leaving. My body got on the plane, planted itself in the Midwest, the East Coast, and other countries, but you always knew if I chose to, I could come back.

I have called other places home that I have been at for many years less and deserve that title much less. I'm sorry for that, but I guess I fall in love too quickly.

What I've avoided saying is that I'm leaving because you feel like the weaker version of me. The me I like a little less, because it would mean I never really went for it, dreamed, or dared. I might come back, but not yet.

You have to know you are the most wonderful and beautiful to me. I would not have traded you for anyone else in the world. You gave me Pacific Coast Highway drives, late night beach adventures, redwood forest hikes, and, dare I say it, some of the best coffee and food I've had in my life. You gave me my entire childhood, friends, and memories. You taught me to appreciate my culture, filled my life with the most inspiring people, and pushed me.

I saw the ugly, dark parts that make it tough to love you some days. It's not what I first think of, but I understand you would not be you without it. I admire other people who have shared my experiences with you and immediately bond with them. No matter where else we are, we remember you. We remember why we left.

Most people spend their whole lives trying to get to you. It's not that I have forgotten, it's not that I won't ever be back, but know that I always miss you most.

Friends or Strangers?

It's been too long to say hi or how are you anymore,
too uncomfortable to want to,
too busy,
but I do wonder occasionally and hope you are okay.
What are you up to?
How are you doing?
What's new?
All silly questions I don't really want answered,
because if we passed by each other on the street
or rode on the same subway car, would you even recognize me?

It's been what, a couple of years?
Is anything about us even the same?
It might be the nostalgia or liquor talking,
but when do we stop being friends with someone
and become strangers?
When are they finally not a part of our lives?
Maybe it's when it stops being so easy to see each other
and when one of us decides to stop catching up
and when we enter different stages of our lives —
or maybe, we never fully become strangers again.

If we once knew each other, are we forever considered friends?
All wishful thinking at best.
Oh, how hard it is to let friends turn into strangers again.

Ruler

How will you measure your life?

In smiles
In dollars
In hours lived
In the number of times you did the hard
thing and came out alive.   **1**

In kisses
In laughs
In bottles drank
In the days you couldn't get out of bed but
still did.   **2**

In smells
In hugs
In countries traveled
In the people you lost but still care about.   **3**

In tears
In friends
In meals shared
In the energy you gave to helping and loving.   **4**

In family
In conversations
In memories created
In the work you are inspired to do.   **5**

In words
In pictures
In jokes told
In the people you surrounded yourself with
until the end.

In changes
In lives touched
In movie moments
In all the questions that will never be answered
like this one.

While the World Is Asleep

My computer screen lights up my face,
my pillow props me up,
my phone is tucked safely away.
The streets are empty,
the sky darkens,
the world sleeps.
No expectations,
no responsibilities,
a strange sense of peace
and control.

Why would I want to fall asleep?

Last Rose

I am here,
but you do not see me.
Maybe if I was her,
you would notice
and pick me.

All The Things I Would Have Told You

If you weren't *you*,
if we still talked,

if I could trust you
and find the words,

I would tell you about how good it felt to be doing better
than yesterday,

how strangely sweet the ocean smelt, how I like warm
wind now,

that I laugh a little different now, more guarded but
still hopeful.

I would tell you I'm thinking about getting a tattoo,

maybe of some clouds or my favorite place in the world,

how I'm still planning on moving *there* (I even looked into
how to get citizenship),

how I just signed my first big girl job, the one I
always wanted,

how I'm more scared to leave home now than before,

and even got into skincare a month ago when I got some
neck acne.

I would tell you I don't wear night contacts anymore, how
my friend and I fought for the first time but it's okay now,

how I just heard about the redwood forests burning
and cried,

all the people I met, rewrote our memories with, and made
more with,

and how grateful I am that I found poetry.

I would want to share what I did today,
how I'm doing,
where I'm going,
but I've accepted that there will be many things I will
never tell you.

coming of age

when is it that point
we become just a little too old
to do stupid things,
and life is no longer
like a coming of age film?

have the biggest challenges we will face
already passed?

Last Time

Can we ever really know
when it will be the last time?

I want to know

the last time I will see something so beautiful it makes me want to cry,
the last time I get so lost in something I forget everything else in the world,
the last time I have my breath taken away by an orange-hued sky.

If I had known it would be the last time I would see her,
I could have told her not to be afraid and that she was so loved
and that I would see her again someday.
A gut-wrenching thought that

I don't get to know

the last words I will say to everyone,
the last moments I will spend in my favorite places,
the last time I will see a person.

Is it too much to ask,
to know?

The Tipping Point

Did that just happen?

We stare at the black hole, the words we finally mustered to
say to you echoing in the silence.
I wish I could take it back, but at the same time,
the churn of a million exhausted butterflies in my stomach
reminds me I can't.

It had to be said.

We had avoided—hell, even *fought* our moments
of courage—
to say how we felt, what you did wrong, and what we
wanted to change.

We went back and forth until we cried to be heard,
until the words finally fell out of my mouth.

Even if it hurt, it came from a place so pure and good that I
could not hate it,
and I wished you didn't either.
But here we are, past the tipping point,
and your silence thuds loudly.

We saw you for who you were,
we loved you despite it,
we took the leap of faith to open up to you
and fell.

When I see the tipping point next time,
I won't be scared to go past it again.

11 PM

I would rather be alone
than be with you

When She Let Go

She imprisoned herself to the cliff's edge,
the tips of her fingers barely hanging on,
afraid to look down, unable to let go.

She was too weak to pull herself back up,
so she grasped for straws
until no choice was left and the rocks gave way.

She pitied herself,
uncertain, destructive, changed,
not ready.

She knew it had to end but didn't know how;
the agony had become an addictive hedonic treadmill,
but end it she did.

And with it, a strange calm swept through her.
She breathed again in the painful silence,
broken but better.

some good ends

There are some good ends that feel like sunsets,
beautiful for just what they are.

A song so wonderful you have to go back and listen,
a book you didn't even realize you were at the end of,
a school year finished and the feeling of freedom,
a day that leaves you tired but was productive,
a bad marriage ended, a job you've grown out of quit,
and every end of mourning and start of healing.

Roses and Peaches

It was all roses and peaches
until I never heard from you again.

A While Too Long

It's been just long enough since we last talked
that I feel like we've lost touch. How long until we can't
call ourselves close friends anymore?

For all the time we spend on our screens, we could
have called
or checked in, but every time I considered it,
the thoughts spilled over and I decided it could wait.

The wait grew the chasm between us
and kept me wondering
why I never heard from you first.

And so I stopped waiting,
even while wishing that I never let a while
turn into a while too long.

Bad at Goodbyes

I would travel oceans if you said you needed me,
burn bridges if you said you wanted me,
dress up like a fool if you said hello again.

I think about our endless conversations and laughs
that left us gasping for air, blasting songs that made us feel
like we were dancing on water, escaping

the monotony of our suburban lives with long drives
to everywhere and nowhere, our arms against open windows,
feeling the warm summer wind blow against our flushed faces.

I don't know how we got here, where the beginning
of the end started, when we drifted so
far apart we were no longer *us*.

Maybe it was when we no longer laughed the same,
the conversations no longer flowed, and the music
became like white noise.

I grasped for straws, wanting to still share the everyday,
the little moments with you. I wanted those nights and
calls to never end—but I knew this was coming.

I am no longer the same, like you. We were young and
held on
too long, too tightly. Until one day
I blinked and it all went cold.

We let go.
Sometimes I find myself in your passenger seat again,
just so I don't ever have to say
goodbye.

here we are again

I see myself in you,
perhaps that's why I loved you.
why I understand you.
why I forgive you.

Letting go comes in waves. Sometimes, I get a pit in my stomach when I hear your name. Sometimes, I panic when I see the cards you gave me and the pictures. Sometimes, I hear a lyric or recall the promise we gave to be in each other's lives for life, and my heart breaks all over again. I remind myself I cannot lose something that what was not meant to be. But you don't even know I'm writing this and you wouldn't know this is for you. No one here even knows about you. No one would think this is about you. So I put the thoughts aside and let us drift apart.

Fade Into the Dark

The more you cling,
the more they drift.

You watch as it begins,
the time lengthens,
things feel different,
and nothing you do
can change what you
know will come.

Some people say
there is no greater pain
than watching the one you love
slowly fade into the dark.

Paris in the Winter

Streets glistening, wet
with rain, as if the city
knew that everything had changed.

Timeless

At the end of the day,
time will not stop
even for you.

Empty Nest

The mother blinks for a moment
and her children are grown,
heads taller than she remembers.
To her, the house still echoes with laughter and her two
children running around,
bumping into walls, as she cleans toys scattered around
the room.
Three stuffed bears, two Lego sets, one baby blanket.
Were they not crying at her leaving for work not long ago?

This was always going to happen.

No more children's books to read or practices to drive
them to. No more music lessons or summer camps.
Her worries,
now said over the phone, fall on deaf ears,
and she sees glimpses of her children's lives from photos
and hears slivers through ten-minute phone calls.

This was always going to happen.

Her children have traded video games for work
laptops, lunch boxes for lunch orders, and saving quarters
for paying rent. They have left band T-shirts for dress
shirts
and dolls for conference calls. They have moved states to
chase
what they have always talked about.

This was always going to happen.

She watches as her children leave again from home,
suitcase luggage in hand, the holidays over.
It is just as hard this time to watch them shut the car door,
knowing her children love her
but they have to go.

Obituaries

They live on in your memories,
look down on you from above,
their laugh echoes as you remember
their odd habits and favorite things.
A piece of you rests with them,
but their importance remains
in the person you have become,
and it will always be more than could ever fit
in an obituary.

The Next

Looking at old photos brings a soft smile to my eyes.
Life Before —
dancing until 4 a.m. in underground bars,
friends and multi-generational families gathered to celebrate or grieve,
calendars packed with trips to museums and fairy-tale cities,
endless possibilities with a checklist to complete.

It was about The Next.
The next job,
house,
vacation,
promotion,
relationship,
every step we were told to search for and go after.

Life Now feels like a time capsule,
a time we will look at in the future, retell,
and remember with great sadness and fondness.
A time when we realized The Next had no guarantee,
not in days, weeks or years.

What seemed essential became afterthoughts,
who seemed essential became irrelevant.
Left with masks, dirty dishes, takeout, and notifications,
we realized
no Next is essential.

Epilogue

I got tired of wondering for too long
if you still listen to our favorite song.

Heaven

There was no one happier —
or so we thought,
and all we can hold onto now
is that you are dancing
somewhere in Heaven
and we will see each other soon.

ACKNOWLEDGEMENTS

When I set out to write *Under Clouds & City Lights,* I had no idea how much poetry would speak to me and how inspiring my experiences with the people around me would be to me for each poem. I could not have written this book without everyone who supported me on this journey, and I am especially thankful for everyone who preordered and believed in me before they even saw this book come to life. The overwhelming support and kind words from my friends and loved ones truly re-energized me.

Thank you first and foremost to my family for supporting me along this process – to my mom, Irene Hsueh-Jen Chen, my dad, Roy Dz-Ching Ju, and my sister, Evaline Ju. Thank you to my former piano teacher, Jin-Ye Wang, and my cousin Chu Pin Yen, for contributing so much to preorders. Countless thanks to my editors, Bailee Noella and Angela Ivey, for giving thoughtful feedback and getting me even more excited for publishing. I'd also like to thank my publisher, New Degree Press, and the team there for making all of this possible. Their vote of confidence made a huge difference in getting me finally writing again.

This dream of having my work published and read would not have been possible without you. Thank you for helping to spread a very personally meaningful message about the importance of validating and understanding thoughts and emotions.

www.ingramcontent.com/pod-product-compliance
Lightning Source LLC
LaVergne TN
LVHW012102070526
838200LV00074BA/3960